Date Due

SEP 29			
NOV 13			
NOV 19			
DEC 4			
FEB 5			
FEB 12			
FEB 2			
FEB 9			
MAR 16			
MAY 27			
DEC 6			
SEP 24			
NOV 24			
APR 5 '82			
NOV 17 '82			
APR 3 '84			
⑬	PRINTED IN U. S. A.		

The FIRST BOOK of
THE LONG ARMISTICE

★★ The FIRST BOOK of ★★

THE LONG ARMISTICE

1919-1939: Europe between wars

by LOUIS L. SNYDER

FRANKLIN WATTS, INC.
575 Lexington Avenue, New York 22

THIS BOOK IS FOR

MAXINE SNYDER

O judgment! thou art fled to brutish beasts,
And men have lost their reason.
        —SHAKESPEARE, Julius Caesar. Act iii. Sc. 1

War, war is still the cry, — "war even to the knife!"
        —BYRON, Childe Harold's Pilgrimage. Canto i. Stanza 86

Fondly do we hope, fervently do we pray, that this mighty
scourge of war may speedily pass away.
        —ABRAHAM LINCOLN, Second Inaugural Address,
        March 4, 1865

CONTENTS

German soldiers in camouflaged helmets about to leave for the front. They wear flowers given them by cheering crowds of young women.

Photo from European

THE HERITAGE OF WORLD WAR I

JUNE 23, 1919. One by one, the German delegates left the Hall of Mirrors at Versailles, near Paris, where they had just been forced to sign the peace treaty that ended World War I. One delegate turned to a reporter and said angrily:

"We'll see you again in twenty years!"

Seldom in history has there been a more accurate prediction than this one made in the bitterness of defeat. The Germans went to war again on September 1, 1939, exactly twenty years, two months, and seven days after the signing of the treaty.

World War I was fought for four years, from 1914 to 1918. On one side were the Allied Powers (Great Britain, France, Russia, the United States, and Italy) and on the other the Central Powers (Germany, Austria-Hungary, Bulgaria, and Turkey). It was a tragic story of blood and agony. It began the century of global, or total, war.

World War I was a war in which millions of men dug into the ground like moles and fought from trenches. It was a war of artillery duels, of battles between monster tanks, of clouds of poison gas drifting across "no-man's-land." It was a war of deadly machine guns, of planes crazily spinning in "dogfights," of lurking U-boats. It was a war of "sea rat" against "land rat," Great Britain against Germany.

On November 11, 1918, when the armies of the Central Powers were falling apart, the opposing countries signed an armistice. World War I had lasted 1,565 days. More than 65,000,000 men took part in it, of whom 13,000,000 died in action in the blood-soaked mud, or later of their wounds. More than 22,000,000 were wounded; 7,000,000 disabled; 5,000,000 missing.

More than twice as many men were killed in World War I as in all major wars from 1790 to 1913 together, including the wars of Napoleon, the Crimean War, the Danish-Prussian War, the Austro-Prussian War, the American War Between the States, the Franco-Prussian War, the Boer War, the Russo-Japanese War, and the Balkan Wars.

World War I cost 400 billion dollars in ruined property on land and

1

President Woodrow Wilson talks to victorious American troops at Chaumont, France, on Christmas, 1918.

sea. Four great empires were smashed: the Russian, the Austro-Hungarian, the Turkish, and the German.

Europe had taken a vicious beating. It was scraped bare. Gone was the glamor and glory of the early days when young men marched singing off to battle. People were tired and unhappy. And it seemed there was to be no end to their misery. In 1918, a terrible flu epidemic struck. The French said it started in Spain; the Spanish said it broke out in France; the Americans said it came from eastern Europe. By the time the formal peace treaty was signed, the disease had spread around the world, killing millions of people. It was one of the three worst scourges of infection in history.

Two voices spoke to a tired Europe. From Woodrow Wilson, twenty-eighth President of the United States, came words of hope: "It will now be our fortunate duty to assist by example . . . and material aid . . . a just democracy throughout the world." This was Wilson's call for a free world.

From Soviet Russia came the voice of Lenin demanding world revolution. He wanted the world to belong to one class — the workers. He called for a war between the classes, repeating the words of Karl Marx's *Communist Manifesto*: "Workingmen of the world unite; you have nothing to lose but your chains!"

Two great ideas now came into conflict — *democracy* (rule by the people) and *dictatorship* (one-man rule).

The years from 1919 to 1939 were not years of peace at all — they were years of truce, a long Armistice between two terrible wars.

More than four thousand hungry children, many of them homeless, lined up for free food daily at this Warsaw, Poland, "feeding kitchen" in 1920.

Photo from European

Delegates from thirty-two victorious nations meet in the Hall of Mirrors at Versailles to draft the peace treaty, January, 1919.

Photo from European

THE TREATY OF VERSAILLES

THE YEAR WAS 1919. The war was over and it was time to make the peace. Delegates and experts from thirty-two victor nations met at Paris on January 18, 1919 to draft a peace treaty. But the losers — Germany, Austria-Hungary, Bulgaria and Turkey — were not invited to attend.

The Big Four at Versailles. From left to right: Italian Premier Orlando; British Prime Minister Lloyd George; French Prime Minister Clemenceau; and American President Woodrow Wilson.

It was not an easy task to bring peace. In the victor nations there was still bitter hatred for the Germans because of the way they had fought the war. They had killed hostages, executed women, sunk ships without warning. The winners wanted not only peace but revenge.

At first the meeting was led by the Big Four — President Woodrow Wilson of the United States; Premier Georges Clemenceau of France; Prime Minister David Lloyd George of Great Britain; and Premier Vittorio Orlando of Italy. Premier Orlando got angry one day and left the meeting, fully expecting to be asked to come back. But no one called him. The Big Four became the Big Three.

The most important voice of the Big Three was that of President Wilson, the first American President to cross the ocean during his term of office. Wilson was met with joy and prayers by the peoples of Europe. He was the great leader, the "Messiah," who would bring peace to a war-torn world.

France's Premier Clemenceau looked like a fierce old walrus, but he was called "The Tiger." "There are only two races," he growled, "the human race and the German race!" And again: "When I die, bury me standing up marching like a soldier against Germany!" He wanted a hard peace. The Germans, he said, had planned the war for forty years. They had started it. Pay them back for what they had done!

Prime Minister Lloyd George had just been reelected to office. He had promised the British people that he would "hang the Kaiser" between two telephone poles — one in London and one in New York. He would make Germany pay for the war, "shilling for shilling, ton for ton." He would "squeeze the lemon until the pips squeak."

Delegates from defeated Germany arrive at Versailles in 1919 carrying their own trunk.
Photo from European

Germany demolishes her munitions at the Krupp works in Essen in accordance with the Versailles Treaty.

Photo from European

In this atmosphere of revenge the American President did his best to work out a fair peace; he asked for an end to secret treaties, freedom of the seas, equality of trade, and reduction of armaments. It was a fine program, but it had no chance of being adopted. Before even the first gun had been fired in 1914, the great powers, anticipating the war to come, had signed treaties, each for its own benefit. In case of an Allied victory, France was to get Alsace and Lorraine; Russia was to take Constantinople. Italy, Germany's ally in 1914, had joined the Allies in 1915 with the promise that she would be awarded more land. Now the winners awaited their spoils of war. They would not be denied by the American President.

By the Treaty of Versailles Germany lost one-eighth of her land, 6,500,000 people, and all her colonies. She had to accept an Allied army of occupation in the Rhineland for fifteen years. To make sure that Germany would not go to war again, her army was limited to 100,000 men. There would be no draft for more soldiers. The German navy was cut to six battleships, six light cruisers, twelve destroyers, and twelve torpedo boats. Germany could have no more U-boats, no air force, no poison gas. The German General Staff was abolished. Kaiser Wilhelm II and other war leaders were to be tried for war crimes (the Kaiser escaped to Holland and was never brought to trial).

7

German delegates listen to Clemenceau at Versailles, 1919.

The Germans were not asked to sign the Treaty of Versailles; they were told to sign it. If they refused, the Allies warned them, their country would be torn apart. The ceremony took place on June 23, 1919, in the Hall of Mirrors in the Trianon Palace in Versailles, near Paris. In this very same hall, forty-eight years earlier, at the end of the Franco-Prussian War in 1871, a victorious Germany had proclaimed her empire, the Second German Reich. Now France held the whip over her old enemy. Revenge was in the very air.

The Germans were sure that, by the terms of the peace, the Allies meant to destroy them utterly. This was not justice, they said, but bitterness and hate. Never would they forget it.

The Germans never did forget. One German in particular, a German by adoption only, a loud, vulgar little man with a sick mind, was to keep the memory of Versailles virulently alive. Adolf Hitler had risen no higher than lance corporal in the German army during World War I. After the war he shouted that he, and he alone, would break "the chains of Versailles." As Nazi dictator of all Germany in 1933, he would soon lead the Germans into a second worldwide war in which they would be smashed down again.

8

THE LEAGUE OF NATIONS

IN SOME 3,457 years of recorded history there have been 3,230 years of war, only 227 years of peace. Yet decent men have long dreamed of a world without war. After the horror and bloodshed of World War I, reasonable human beings have wanted some kind of world order set up to avoid future wars.

The idea of a League of Nations to handle all affairs of common concern came from Jan Smuts, a South African military and political leader. The man who worked hardest for the League was the American President, Woodrow Wilson.

At first the members of the League were only the victor powers. Germany was accepted in 1926 and Russia in 1934. The League had three major units. In the Assembly each nation had three delegates but only one vote. The Assembly talked over matters, but did not make laws. The Council, at first, had nine members (five great powers with permanent seats; and four members from smaller nations). The Council could make plans to reduce armaments and settle disputes between countries. The Secretariat was a staff of officials who did all the written work.

The League of Nations opens on September 26, 1924, to propose an international conference on armaments. In the center of the photograph is the British delegation, with the British Prime Minister on the extreme right.
Wide World Photo

Jan Christian Smuts.

The rules of the League of Nations were in the covenant, or written constitution. Two articles in the covenant were of great importance: Article 10 said that no member of the League could be attacked and its land taken away; Article 16 held that should any member of the League go to war in disregard of its duties to the League, all other members would cut off trade with that nation (sanctions).

The League of Nations handled more than thirty serious but small disputes. For example, Finland and Sweden both laid claim to the Aaland Islands, which lay between them in the Gulf of Bothnia. The League settled the matter by giving the islands to Finland, but she had to respect Swedish rights in the islands. This was the kind of wise action that stopped wars.

Sad to say, the League had some serious weaknesses. The failure of the United States to become a member was a severe blow to it. Certainly the League suffered a loss when it refused, for some years, to admit Germany and Russia. These two were great powers on the Continent. The nations that did join the League gave it only lukewarm support. Above all, they did not want to give up their arms. This was disastrous. Had all the members given the League their warm and enthusiastic support, they might have made it a more vital body than it was.

Although the League took good care of the little disputes, it proved to be too weak when the big ones arose. It failed to halt Japan's invasion of Manchuria in 1931, Italy's conquest of Ethiopia in 1935-36, and the Spanish Civil War in 1936-39.

The League did the very best it could in many ways. It gave money to needy states in Central Europe and the Balkans. It did highly important work in preventive medicine, in stopping the traffic in women, children, and opium, in the struggle against slavery and forced labor. Each year it received reports on mandates — colonies held before the war by Germany and Turkey and now guarded by the victor powers. The League also watched out for the rights of 30,000,000 minority peoples, such as the Poles in Germany, the Germans in Czechoslovakia, and the Jews in many lands.

Perhaps the greatest value of the League was as a vehicle of propaganda for a true world society. It spread the idea of cooperation among nations and, more than any other agency, helped to make people aware of world conditions and problems. It was an advance over times past just to have men from all over the world meet at one table so that they might come to know one another and share each other's thoughts.

The idea of an association of nations was old, but the actuality of the League of Nations was new. The major aim of the League was to keep the peace. It failed in the end to do this because it could be only what the nations made of it — nothing less and nothing more. But just the same it was a vital first step in building a system of world order.

Today we have the United Nations, which, in its purpose, its principles, and its methods, bears at every point the mark of the League of Nations. The Security Council, the Assembly, and the Secretariat of the

11

Blairsville Joint
Junior High School

The arms parley opens at Geneva.

United Nations, all are modeled on the League of Nations. The fact that at the end of World War II the United Nations was desired and approved by the civilized peoples of the world shows the wisdom of the men who planned the League of Nations.

Man learns by doing. The League of Nations taught us how to find the road to a world society. The United Nations carries on. Perhaps we shall one day have a world in which there is no war.

THE SEARCH FOR PEACE AND SECURITY

BEFORE 1914 THE NATIONS of Europe felt that their security lay in union with other nations by a signed contract or pact called a treaty. In such treaties they promised to defend each other in case of war. As

World War I approached, the nations of Europe believed themselves protected by two major sets of treaties: the secret Triple Alliance (Germany, Austria-Hungary, and Italy) and the Triple Entente (England, France, and Russia). But war came.

After 1919, the nations of Europe seemed about to try a new way to keep the peace. The old way had not prevented war; perhaps the League of Nations would help. But the world had learned little from the past. The loser nations, angry with the peace treaties, did what they could to avoid paying for the war. The victor powers were afraid of new attacks. Old fears gave way to new fears. Soviet Russia and the Western nations distrusted each other. The French feared further attacks by the Germans. The Germans wanted revenge against the winner nations.

How could the nations find safety in a jungle world of hate and fear? They returned to the old system of treaties. Three new sets of military pacts — French, Russian, and Italian — were set up.

The French feared the Germans above all. "We live just across the Rhine from them and we have had to fight them for a thousand years!" The French set up their own system: pacts with Belgium (1920); Poland (1922); Czechoslovakia (1924); Romania (1926); Yugoslavia (1927); Russia (1933); and England (1938). They helped form the "Little Entente" between Czechoslovakia, Yugoslavia, and Romania (all three carved out in part from the old Austro-Hungarian Empire).

That was still not enough for the French. Between their country and Germany they built a huge underground fort called the Maginot Line. Hundreds of miles long, it was an amazing array of big guns, barracks, railroads, hospitals — all under the ground! Frenchmen believed it to be impregnable, but when Hitler attacked France in 1940, he simply sent his troops through Belgium into France around the Maginot Line, as though he were executing an end run in football.

The Russians, too, were afraid. They had been weakened by huge losses in the war. They wanted to defend their revolution against a hostile world. They, too, made a series of pacts with their neighbors.

The Italians, angered by the peace treaty that had given them so few spoils of war, also made a series of friendship pacts with other nations.

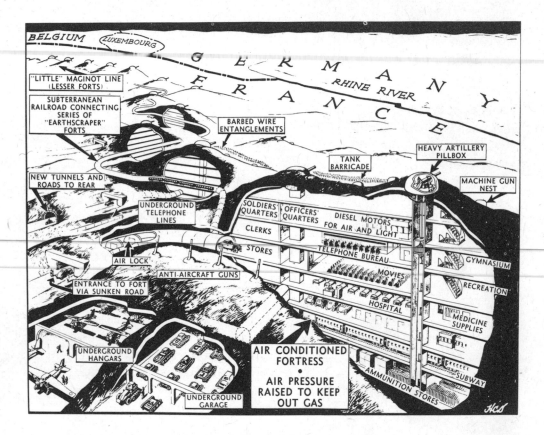

Diagram of the Maginot Line, France's underground fortress.

One of the danger spots between France and Germany was the Rhineland. In October, 1925, France, Germany, and England signed a treaty at Locarno, a little town in Switzerland whose cooing white doves were symbols of peace. At Locarno, the Germans gave up their claims to Alsace and Lorraine, the provinces between France and Germany over which the two nations had fought for centuries. Now, the French said, they could be friends with the Germans. The Germans then joined the League of Nations.

The whole world took heart at this new "Spirit of Locarno." People spoke of a new era of peace and good will on earth.

On August 27, 1928, the Kellogg-Briand Peace Pact, or the Paris Peace Pact, was signed by fifteen nations (by 1933 it was signed by sixty-two nations). All these nations agreed to give up war. All said that they would settle their disputes by talking it over, *never by going to war*. All agreed to "renounce war as an instrument of national policy."

Once again, people took hope. Decent men said that war was a savage thing unfit for human society. They hoped the day would come when people would consider war as out of date as cannibalism.

Men of good will did their best to cut down armaments, the tools of war. In 1921-22 the American President, Warren Harding, called the Washington Naval Conference. The great naval powers agreed to stop making battleships for ten years and to cut down their other warships in this ratio: United States, 5; Great Britain, 5; Japan, 3; France, 1.67; and Italy, 1.67. There were also other meetings to reduce the number of warships. But no one seemed to be happy with this idea of cutting down strength.

Other efforts were made to abolish armaments on land, weapons such as tanks, bombing planes, and big guns. But all these attempts failed. Too many leaders felt: "We live in a world in which only power is respected. If we are strong, no one will dare attack us. Hence, we must be strong."

Others said that when arms are built up the chances are that some day they will be used.

The arms were used — to the great sorrow of mankind.

15

DEMOCRACY VERSUS DICTATORSHIP

AFTER WORLD WAR I, two ways of life — democracy and dictatorship — clashed head on.

The word democracy comes from two Greek words, *dēmos* (the people) and *kratein* (rule). It means, in the words of Abraham Lincoln, "government of the people, by the people, and for the people." Great gains in democracy have come only because people fought for them, as in the English Revolution of 1688, the American Revolution of 1776, and the French Revolution of 1789.

The first quality of democracy is freedom. A democracy is an *open society*. People in a democracy have the right to speak freely. They may read what they like. They may gather in groups to make their voices heard. They have the right to trial by jury. They may practice their religion as they wish.

This does not mean that everything in a democracy is perfect and that it is a paradise on earth. Not at all. There are ideals, or goals to which the democratic man aspires — but they are ideals set in his laws. The right of every person, regardless of creed or color, to life, liberty, and the pursuit of happiness, is a right guaranteed by law in a democracy. The fact that some people refuse to honor these laws does not mean that democracy itself is weak, but only that *some* people in it are weak or ignorant.

The great democratic countries after World War I were Great Britian (a democratic monarchy), France, and the United States (democratic republics). Most of the small new countries became democratic republics. A republic is a country ruled by the people through their elected delegates, such as a president and congressmen. Both a republic and a monarchy can be democracies. But a republic can never have a king at its head.

Before World War I most European countries were monarchies, ruled by a king or queen. After World War I, among twenty-six countries there were only eight monarchies left.

Democracy seemed to be on the march after 1919. But in those hard times there came another way of life — dictatorship. Dictatorship means that supreme rule in a country is taken over by one man or one party. A dictator is a master who holds absolute rule over a people. He calls himself The Leader — *El Caudillo* in Spanish, *Der Fuehrer* in German, *Il Duce* in Italian. Sometimes he calls himself chief commander of the military forces, or *Generalissimo,* as Franco did in Spain.

Dictatorship is as old as history; it is just another word for tyranny. The dictator or tyrant wants one thing above all — power. He wants absolute control of the nation. He will not let anyone or anything stand in his way. He will crush all opponents without mercy. He will have the people watched by his secret police. He will see to it that all young people learn to glorify his name. He will make his country ready for war. The one thing he cannot do is to stand still. He must always push ahead for new glory, new victories.

The dictator runs the total life of the people. That is why this way of life is called totalitarianism. Unlike democracy, it is a *closed society.*

Following World War I, there were two main forms of dictatorship in Europe — fascism and communism. Both denied the people freedom.

WHY COMMUNISM? WHY FASCISM?

Most young people of today, if they are shown pictures of those tragic years between the two great wars, find it hard to understand why intelligent people could accept the ideas and ways of life they did. Young Germans are horrified when they see films of the Hitler days — pictures of storm troopers beating people on the streets, of Nazis burning books, the unspeakable horrors of the concentration camps. How could these things happen? How could seemingly decent men turn to dictators? How could civilized people go berserk?

These are not easy questions to answer. First we must look at the political, economic, and emotional climate that made possible the rise of communism and fascism. The great nations of the world seemed sick. No one knew how to cure them. In Britain and France democracy was working only lamely. Before 1914 the parliaments of Europe had tried to solve their problems by a flood of oratory. But World War I, its aftermath, and the Great Depression raised new and acute problems. The old political routines seemed helpless and outmoded. Something else, many people believed, was needed to master the situation.

Two systems — communism and fascism — looked to some like the only answers. Although they were quite similar in many respects, they had different appeals. Why did some nations go communist? Why did others go fascist?

There was nothing new about communism. Communism, or something like it, had been threatening ever since the European revolutions of 1848. There had been many kinds of communism. When it finally came to Russia in 1917 it came in a highly intolerant form. Europeans were prepared for it. Conservatives and liberals were against it from the start. And democratic Socialists, after a period of hesitation, swung around against it. It was not easy to judge what the Russians intended to do, but the outlines of their system were clear to both friend and foe.

Many men of good will turned to communism because they were confused, helpless, and despairing and they thought that anything was better than the present world. When they found that the communism of Lenin and Stalin was just another form of tyranny, it was too late. They had to go along with it or be purged.

Fascism, on the other hand, came as a great surprise. In this case there was no warning. World War I set in motion a true mass movement. Masses of people, hit by inflation and depression, turned to fascism because it promised a way out of their troubles.

People became Fascists because fascism seemed to give them the answers they wanted. It appealed to all sides. It spoke the language of socialism, but it defended large fortunes. It seemed to be revolutionary, but it carefully defended property and the old traditions, which made it reactionary. It was called "the radicalism of the Right." It brought out all the old symbols of "loyalty," "honor," "nation," and gave them new vigor by wrapping them in brutality and melodrama.

18

German Communists in Berlin, wearing gas masks, protest against gas warfare in an anti-war demonstration.
Photo from European

Decent people in Mussolini's Italy, Hitler's Germany, and Franco's Spain honestly believed they were being good patriots by supporting the new "Wave of the Future." They were hypnotized by the dictators' speeches, the marching bands, the goose-stepping troops. Their minds were brainwashed by propaganda, parades, and circuses. Young people were entranced by the rumbling drums, the joyous music, the songs of victory.

When they awakened, it was too late. Whole nations were enslaved by dictators and their parties who had power and intended to keep it. People had been fooled by a sham and a fraud. Instead of lifting their nations out of confusion and despair, the dictators led them straight into war and misery.

BRITAIN IN THE INTERWAR YEARS

GERMANY WAS BEATEN! London and the little villages of England greeted the war's end with joy. People danced in the streets and sang in the pubs. Now Britain would be, as wartime Prime Minister David Lloyd George had said, "a land fit for heroes."

For many years the little island off the coast of Europe had been the workshop of the world. She had been the world's richest banker, the world's largest trader. London had been the hub of the world's commerce. Surely, with victory, the British people would go on to an even better, richer life.

But this was not to be. Britain had been hit hard by the war. She had lost a million men on the battlefields and in the seas. Many who came back from the war found no work. Taxes were twice as high as in 1913. Conditions went from bad to worse.

During the war England's foreign trade had fallen off. She had lost two of her best customers on the Continent — Germany and Russia. Both were now too poor to buy British goods. The British coal trade had to compete with the cheap coal that had been turned over to the French and Italians as part payment by Germany on reparations. British coal mines became idle. The shipyards, too, began to close down. Where the French could live largely on their own agriculture if they had to, the British were completely dependent on foreign trade.

Britain was ripe for political trouble. In rough times such as these, other peoples turned to dictators, but not Britain. She was saved by her political system, British democracy, one of her great gifts to mankind.

At the head of the state was a king, who reigned but did not rule. He stood aloof from party politics. He was a symbol of national and imperial unity.

The kingdom was led by a prime minister, whose term of office depended on a majority of votes in the House of Commons (similar to the House of Representatives in the United States Congress). The members of the House of Commons were elected by the people. The upper body, the House of Lords, composed of the aristocrats and nobility, was at one time the more important of the two legislative bodies, but its powers had been cut down over the centuries until it had become little more than a debating society.

A part of the secret of British political success was the fact that men of high ability were attracted to public service. British politicians in the House of Commons never turned to violence in debates. They merely

20

sat down and talked things over. They believed in compromise — give a little here and take a little there. This was the spirit that saved British democracy.

There were three main political parties in Britain — the Conservatives, Liberals, and Laborites.

The Conservative party looked to the past. It wanted to conserve, or hold fast, to what was best; it was slow to adopt new ideas. The Conservatives believed in private enterprise, or capitalism. They did not want the government to take away the historic liberties of the people. They asked for high tariffs to protect British industry. They wanted a strong army and navy to protect the Empire.

The Liberal party, once the second strongest, began to lose its place after World War I. Liberals believed in individual freedom. They wanted free trade because that would keep down the price of goods. They said that they were the party of the middle, for neither the rich nor the poor, but for Britain.

The Laborites, who became the second major political party, had the same aim as Socialists the world over. They wanted the state to own the means of production. They wanted the government, not the capitalists, to run the factories on behalf of the people. But they did not like to be called Socialists. They were against class warfare, revolution, and the atheism of a Marxian Socialism. The other fellow, they said, also had a right to be heard. "We are *democratic* Socialists!" they said.

The Conservatives were in power most of the time between 1919 and 1939. Their leader, Stanley Baldwin, heavy set, square-jawed, slow-thinking, served three times as prime minister. The Laborites were twice in office. The first Labor ministry, January, 1924, to November, 1924, headed by James Ramsay MacDonald, was voted down because the people feared it was too friendly with Soviet Russia; the second Labor ministry stayed in power from 1929 to 1931.

Those were dreary years. Trade fell off badly, and millions were jobless. No longer was the proud slogan, "Made in Britain," seen in markets all over the world.

The British asked the United States to cancel the war debt of $4,000,000,000, which had been lent to them during the war years, but the American President, Calvin Coolidge, would not consider such a thing. "They hired the money, didn't they?" he asked.

Britain recovered slowly but steadily. She did not regain her high place of 1914, but conditions in the country became better. Unemployment was cut down, but the problem of poverty was not solved.

In 1936 came a great political crisis. On the death of King George V his son, the Prince of Wales, became Edward VIII, but he refused to be crowned without the right to marry an American divorcée. The Church of England, of which the king is the head, does not permit Britain's ruler to marry a divorced woman. Prime Minister Stanley Baldwin angrily saw to it that Edward VIII gave up his throne in favor of his younger brother, who became George VI in 1937. Baldwin, feeling that he had saved the monarchy, then resigned.

Britons at this time did not know that all Europe was in peril. Hitler and Mussolini were rattling their weapons, but the average Briton was thoroughly tired of war talk and refused to listen. Yes, he hated nazism, but what could he do about it? Many Britons signed peace pledges.

Edward VIII, uncrowned King of England, at the time of his abdication.
Wide World Photo

Winston Churchill in 1937.
Wide World Photo

Students at Oxford University swore that they would never again fight for king and country. Men and women pledged that they would march unarmed between armies in any future war and thus die for peace.

Meanwhile, a Briton with an iron heart and a golden voice tried to warn his people. "Do not forget," said Winston Churchill, "that the most warlike people in Europe, the Germans, are being welded into a tremendous fighting machine."

Few listened to Churchill in 1938 when he said:

I have watched this famous island descending to a dark gulf.... If we study the history of Rome and Carthage, we can understand what happened and why.... Historians a thousand years hence will be baffled by the mystery of our affairs. They will never understand how it was that a victorious nation, with everything in hand, suffered themselves to be brought low, and to cast away all that they had gained by measureless sacrifice and absolute victory — gone with the wind!

Now the victors are the vanquished, and those who threw down their arms in the field and sued for an armistice are striding on to world mastery.

23

FRANCE BETWEEN TWO WARS

WORLD WAR I took a fearful toll in France. More than a million Frenchmen died on the battlefields. One tenth of the country, the northeastern corner, lay in ruins. Huge textile mills were destroyed. Coal mines were flooded, small villages wiped out by shellfire. Wells were filled up or contaminated, orchards were cut down, and railway lines were smashed. The once rich area was covered with rusty barbed wire, shell holes, and debris.

Little wonder then that the people of postwar France were tense and worried. The army was restless. City workers went hungry for bread while the unhappy farmers struggled to repair the ruined farms. The middle class feared the spread of communism. Most of all, however, Frenchmen wanted to be sure that the Germans would not attack them again.

The French, despite their troubles, were true to the democratic way of life. Most of them were still proud that the great slogan, "Liberty, Equality, and Fraternity" could be traced back to their own Revolution of 1789. Freedom-loving as they were, they hoped to avoid both communism and fascism.

The Third French Republic was a democracy, with a weak president, a legislature of two houses, and a cabinet. Unlike Britain, which had a two-party system, France had many political parties. To get a majority of votes in the lower house, the Chamber of Deputies, a dozen or more parties would get together in a bloc. The government was changed frequently. Since it began in 1875, the Third French Republic had had more than a hundred different cabinets! The French said that this was democratic because it showed the will of the people. Others called it a sign of weakness.

Between the two world wars, three blocs fought for political power:

The first was the *National Bloc* (1919-24), a union of conservatives of the Right, middle-of-the roaders, and a few radicals on the Left. Its leader was Raymond Poincaré, a patriot who had been president during World War I and who now asked that the Germans be punished severely.

24

One of the French villages in the vicinity of Verdun destroyed in World War I.
Photo by Paul Thompson

The *Left Bloc* (1924-26) was more radical. It included the Center and the Left. Its leaders were Édouard Herriot, the popular one-time mayor of Lyons, and Aristide Briand, an old radical who was willing to forgive the Germans and be friendly with them.

The *Popular Front* (1936-38) was a union of all Left groups led by Léon Blum. This was something new in French politics. For the first time, Socialists and Communists, who hated each other, tried to work together.

One of the great problems was how to save the French franc. The Germans were supposed to pay for the damage to France. But how was France to get money from Germany? Without waiting, the French began to rebuild their towns, factories, and mines. They spent 7 billion dollars and charged it to the Germans. Only a small part was ever paid back. The Germans either did not want to or could not pay.

25

The French money system could not stand the strain. In 1914 the franc was worth twenty cents. In 1926 it slid down to two cents. This was inflation. At this time, thoughtless American tourists would make the French furious by pasting paper francs on their baggage as if they were hotel stickers. By hard work and new taxes the value of the franc was saved.

There was trouble, too, in Alsace and Lorraine. Germans and Frenchmen had been fighting for a long time over these two rich provinces that lie between their two countries. In 1919 the French got them back. But what about the Germans who still lived there? There were disputes over language, religion, political rights, and education of children. The language problem was hard to manage. It was finally solved by teaching the children only French during their first two years of school; after which they could speak either French or German as their parents wished. In 1925 Alsace and Lorraine were made a part of France and were governed from Paris until the Nazi invasion of 1940.

In 1934 came the threat of a Fascist revolt in France. It was started

Workers in the Renault automobile plant go on strike as France is hit by a wave of strikes in 1936.
Photo from European

Anxious crowds in front of the Paris Stock Exchange, July 1, 1937, as the Exchange opens without having established a gold standard.
Photo from European

by the Stavisky scandals. A wealthy playboy, son of a Russian dentist, Serge Alexander Stavisky moved in high circles, gambled with marked cards, forged checks, and spent money lavishly. To pay his debts, he began to steal millions of francs from the city pawnshops of Bayonne.

To avoid arrest, Stavisky fled to the French Alps, where he was found dying in a hut. It was said that he was killed by police to prevent his talking and exposing important political leaders as crooks. There may have been something to this gossip, for Stavisky was friendly with some of the leading members of the government.

The affair provided fine propaganda for the Fascists and other malcontents. *Les Cagoulards* (The Hooded Ones), an armed secret society, called for a return of the monarchy. The king would restore order, they said. The *Croix de Feu* (The Cross of Fire), a group of veterans who claimed a million members, marched on the Chamber of Deputies, broke windows, overturned buses, and beat up Communists. Would there be civil war again?

Paris was in an uproar. All the Left groups — Radicals, Socialists, and

Communists — now joined in a Popular Front to oppose fascism. The rich, who had lost part of their wealth when the franc fell in value, contended with the thousands of workers who had no jobs at all. The trouble was that the world was not buying French products, most of which were luxury items — perfume, fine wines, silks, and fashions. Americans, Britons, and Germans had too many troubles of their own to buy French goods. Poor, almost hopelessly divided, France grew weaker and weaker.

EUROPE AND THE UNITED STATES

WHEN THE UNITED STATES entered the war against Germany and the Central Powers in April, 1917, the German Kaiser, Wilhelm II, said that America could not get enough men to Europe in time to win the war. But within months a million Americans had crossed the Atlantic on a bridge of ships. American help was vital in defeating the Germans.

Before the war the United States owed money to European countries. After the war it became the richest nation on earth. From 1790 to 1940 its population rose from 3,929,214 to 131,669,275. Today, the United States produces more than one-half the total goods made in the world. It has more than one-half the world's total income.

In 1916 Woodrow Wilson, a Democrat, was reelected President of the United States on the slogan "He kept us out of war." In the long run, however, he found it impossible to keep out of Europe's quarrels. In a sense, the world had grown smaller. America did go to war. Afterward, the United States returned to the policy of isolation George Washington had advised in his farewell address — "Keep out of European affairs."

In 1928, with the shadow of the Great Depression of the thirties already falling on the country, Herbert Hoover was elected President of the United States. In 1929 the stock market crashed. Business declined. Millions of men lost their jobs. The government tried, but there seemed to be no hope of avoiding complete disaster.

In 1932 Hoover was defeated for reelection by Franklin Delano

Crowds on the steps of the Sub-Treasury building opposite the New York Stock Exchange on the day of the Wall Street crash.

Wide World Photo

Roosevelt. Telling the people that "We have nothing to fear but fear itself," Roosevelt launched a New Deal, a series of reforms to help what he called "the forgotten man." He put business under strict control, gave help to the jobless and aid to the farmers. He helped small home-owners. He promised people that their money would be safe in the banks. He set up a social security system, so that elderly people could retire in comfort without fear for their future. He put the jobless to work building roads and bridges. Boys of teen age, if they wished, could go to CCC (Civilian Conservation Corps) camps, where they could help to save the country's natural resources.

Slowly, partly under the impact of these emergency measures, the country lifted itself out of hard times.

Some people opposed Roosevelt and his reforms, but farmers, work-

Depression years in the United States. These men, living in a flimsy shack, have sold empty bottles for ten cents and spent the money for potatoes.

Photo from European

ers, and small businessmen approved of his program. He was elected again in 1936, and again in 1940. He was the first and only American President to serve a third term. He died during his fourth term, on April 12, 1945.

The Roosevelt administration was marked not only by a strong and successful domestic policy, but also by a strong foreign policy. Roosevelt called for a world order, friendship with Latin-American countries, and opposition to the dictators. Like Woodrow Wilson, Franklin D. Roose-

Franklin D. Roosevelt accepts the nomination to run for a second term, 1936.

Wide World Photo

velt had hoped to keep the United States out of war, but again, war came. In 1941, America joined the Allied nations in their struggle to preserve the free world.

COMMUNISM IN SOVIET RUSSIA

THERE ARE 8,764,000 square miles of land in Russia. They stretch from the Arctic Ocean to the Black and Caspian seas, from Central Europe to the Pacific Ocean. In the nineteenth century more than 180,000,000 people of varied cultures lived in Russia, and out of every 1,000 of them, more than 800 were peasants. Until 1860, when Czar Alexander II put an end to serfdom, most peasants lived and worked on estates owned by either the nobles or the government. Many were harshly treated, and few were given the opportunity to learn to read and write. The reforms of Nicholas II (1868-1918), last Russian emperor, helped somewhat, but they did not end the peasants' misery. They were still poor, hungry, overworked, and few of them could look forward to anything better.

Civilian Conservation Camp in Rainier National Park, Washington, in 1933.

Wide World Photo

Russian peasant workers return from the field carrying primitive rakes and scythes. One of the Communist government's major concerns was the modernization of Russian farm machinery.

Photo from European

Toward the beginning of the twentieth century, Russia began to develop her industries. Thousands of peasants migrated to the cities in hope of a better life. If anything, life was harder in the city than in the country. While millions of poverty-stricken peasants begged for more land, the city workers cried out for food.

From 1894 to 1917 Russia was ruled by Nicholas II, Emperor and Autocrat of All the Russias, the "Little White Father," to his people. Nicholas loved his country and his family, but he was always in deadly fear of revolution. Ruling with an iron hand, he sent thousands of his protesting subjects into exile in Siberia.

Nicholas had a strong-willed wife, the Czarina Alexandra, who was under the influence of a Siberian monk, a mystic and charlatan named Grigori Rasputin. Coarse, greedy, and unkempt, Rasputin believed that the best way to conquer evil was to give in to it.

The young heir to the throne, the Czarevitch Alexis, was a hemophiliac (a tendency, usually hereditary, to profuse bleeding even from slight wounds). Doctors could not help him. Only the wild monk, Rasputin, who probably had hypnotic powers, was able to soothe the ill and cranky boy. For this reason he gained power over both the Czarina and the Czar.

Russia was among the first nations to become involved in World War I. Her troops fought the German invaders with stubborn courage, but their leaders were weak. From the start, everything went wrong: trains broke down, food vanished from the cities, soldiers threw away their weapons and went home. Russia was beaten badly by the Germans.

In 1917 there were two revolutions in Russia. One was in March (February by the old Russian calendar), the second was in November (October).

Preceding the March revolution there were food riots in Petrograd (formerly St. Petersburg and today called Leningrad). Finally a military uprising swept away Nicholas II and his Romanov dynasty, and a democratic republic under Alexander Kerensky was set up. The new government pledged Russia to fight to the end against Germany and the Central Powers.

Soldiers mingle with the crowds of workmen and citizens during the first hours of the Bolshevik Revolution, 1917.

Photo from European

The news that Russia would fight on brought joy to the Allies. "Russia," said President Wilson, "is now a fit partner for a League of Honor."

But the Russian Republic lasted less than eight months. The story of how it fell is tied up with the life of a stocky little man with slanting eyes, bald head, and a pointed beard. N. Lenin, whose real name was Vladimir Ilich Ulyanov (1870-1924), was the son of a school inspector. (Bolshevik leaders changed their names because they were always being followed by the secret police.) Like his brothers and sisters, Lenin, even as a schoolboy, read revolutionary books. He saw his older brother hanged for trying to kill Czar Alexander III. One day, said young Lenin, "heads would roll." He would make "those vermin" pay for taking his brother's life.

Lenin spent a large part of his early life in exile. In April, 1919, the German High Command, seeking to weaken Russia as much as it could, brought Lenin from his Swiss exile to Russia in a sealed train. Imme-

Armed Bolsheviks gather in front of the Duma, or Russian Parliament.

Nikolai Lenin in the court-
yard of the Kremlin,
about 1923.
Photo from European

diately Lenin took charge of the Bolshevik drive for power. At his elbow
was another veteran exile, Leon Trotsky, whose real name was Lev
Davydovich Bronstein. Trotsky had hurried home from his refuge in
New York to be the brilliant orator of the new revolution. Another
loyal follower of Lenin was the silent but deadly Joseph Stalin whose
real name was Iosif Vissarionovich Dzhugashvili.

The Bolsheviks, or "majority" party members, were a tough, obedient
group of agitators who knew what they wanted and how to get it.
Backed by eighty thousand workers, they pushed their way into the
soviets, or councils of workers and soldiers, that rose in the cities and
villages. They were later to be called Communists.

"Peace! Land! Bread!" was their slogan. And again: "All power to
the Soviets!"

On November 6 and 7, 1917, on orders from Lenin, the Bolsheviks
revolted in Petrograd and other big cities and overthrew the Kerensky
government. These were the famous "ten days that shook the world."

Women strikers parade in Petrograd.

Lenin and his Bolsheviks were fanatics who wanted to make over not only Russia but the whole world. Their plans were based on what they claimed were the basic preachments of the German-born philosopher, Karl Marx:

1. *Capitalism, the private ownership of property,* because of its inconsistencies and contradictions, would wither and die away. In Lenin's view, capitalism and its twin, imperialism, were evils that led only to war.

2. *People would own everything in common* (communism). "From each according to his capacity, to each according to his need."

3. *There would be a dictatorship of the proletariat.* The proletariat, the workers and peasants, would have all power in the government.

All who denied this creed, whether they were inside or outside Russia, were to be opposed. Lenin was sure that all Europe, broken by war, would soon turn to communism.

36

But communism failed to win Europe or the world. At the same time, the world failed to overcome communism in Russia. A bloody civil war began in 1918. The Communist Red Army, led by Trotsky, fought to the death against their enemies, called the "Whites." The Whites, led by officers of the prewar ruling class, were supported by the Allies. Britain, France, the United States, and Japan all sent fighting forces to Russia. The Bolsheviks never forgot this. It helps explain their mistrust of the West.

At this time, when Russia was racked with civil war, Polish armies marched into the Ukraine as far as Kiev. The Russians struck back, sweeping westward to the very gates of Warsaw, and threatened to overrun Poland entirely. But the Poles, with some help from Britain and France, recovered and drove the Russians back. The Poles and the Russians had long hated each other. Now this hatred was sharpened.

The fighting inside Russia was hard and vicious, but by 1921 it was all over. The victory of the revolution was assured. The Red Army had the advantage of a central position, controlling Moscow and Petrograd. What they lacked in arms they made up for in enthusiasm, discipline,

Leon Trotsky, Russian revolutionary leader, in 1919.

Photo from European

and propaganda. The Bolsheviks had promised their Red troops that they would one day own the land if they fought for it. The Whites had had no such "red apple" to dangle before their troops. When the war-weary Allies withdrew their forces, the White counterrevolution staggered and then collapsed.

The November Revolution was supposed to be a clean break with the past, but the old Imperial Russian ideas were hard to erase. "If you have a political enemy, destroy him." Lenin and his Bolsheviks started a reign of terror. Ruthlessly they killed thousands of their enemies. Many Russians fled to other countries. Czar Nicholas II and his family were herded into a cellar and shot down. The old nobility and the middle class were stripped of power and property.

The whole world was shocked by news of the brutal killings inside Russia. To many people communist Russia was a barbaric land of murder and fear.

The U.S.S.R. (Union of Soviet Socialist Republics) was composed at first of seven states, of which the R.S.F.S.R. (Russian Socialist Federated Soviet Republic) was the largest. All men and women workers above the age of eighteen could vote.

Photo from European

Grand Duke Nicholas of Russia.

The real power was the Communist party. In its early days it had 2,500,000 members. The head of the party, the secretary-general, was the real dictator of Soviet Russia.

The new Russia was called "a free Socialist society of the working people of Russia." But there was little freedom in this society. It was said to be a "dictatorship of the proletariat" — but it was not. It was a dictatorship *over* the people. The head of the Communist party — first Lenin, later Stalin — was the dictator.

In old Russia, the *Okhrana*, or secret police, had kept the people in fear of the Czar. Now the Communists had their own secret police, known as the Cheka, later the Gay-Pay-Oo (OGPU), and still later the NKVD. The secret police watched the people like hawks, ever ready to strike on even the suspicion of disloyalty to the party. They would enter homes in the middle of the night and arrest an "enemy of the state." His relatives might never hear from him again.

The Communists, once in power, tried to change Russian society overnight. They called it War Communism (1917-21), meaning that they would introduce communism in one giant step. They seized all the land, factories, mines, railways, banks, and shipyards. Party members, who knew nothing about factories and mines, were detailed to run them.

The result was chaos. Trains broke down. People in the towns went hungry because the farmers refused to give up their food without being paid for it. With a poor harvest came famine, and with famine, epidemics of sickness. Typhus alone killed more than 5,000,000 people. The death toll would have been much higher had not the United States shipped in food and medical supplies.

Soviet Russia was on the verge of collapse. Lenin realized that he could not move too far too fast. He must go back, at least for a while, to the old system. He called it the New Economic Policy (NEP), "taking one step backward in order to take two forward." He allowed the little businessmen to open their shops; he gave the small factories back to their former owners. He permitted the peasants to sell some of their food at a profit.

The results were good. Industry, business, and farming began to rise again.

Now came a series of Five-Year Plans "to overtake and surpass the West." The First Five-Year Plan (1928-33) aimed to increase industry by 130 per cent, farming by about 50 per cent. It had some success. The Second Five-Year Plan (1933-38) tried to produce better goods for the stores. The Third Five-Year Plan (1938-42) sought to bring a complete Communist society.

From the start the Communists paid close attention to schools and education. Adults were taught to read and write. Every child was given the right to go to school. The work was very hard. There were many hours of homework. Young people were taught to be loyal to communism. Everything that helped the communist cause was said to be good; anything which stood in its way was evil.

The teachings of Karl Marx came first in the school books. Students were taught that "wicked capitalism" was the cause of all evil. The work of Marx and Lenin, they were told, was the highest glory of the human race.

After school hours and on holidays the boys and girls were kept busy in the Young Pioneers. Later they joined the Young Communist League (*Komsomol*). Boys from twelve to fifteen were given military training. The highest honor for a young person was to be accepted as a member of the Communist party.

Russian society was changed. A citizen's first loyalty was not to his family but to the working class. Most women went to work; their children were placed in nursery schools for the day. Workers were given free medical care, free vacations, books, music, and movies at low cost, and pensions.

The Communists said that there was no God, that "religion was the opiate of the people." Churches they tore down or changed into clubhouses and museums. "Godless societies" sprang up. Preachers, priests, and monks were left to become beggars, while children were taught to laugh at religion. The state, they were told, is the Supreme Being.

The legal system was changed. If one man killed another in a sudden

40

Joseph Stalin with officials of the Russian Soviet Government, 1927.

Photo from European

fit of anger, he was treated as sick and given a short jail sentence. But if a man was proven guilty of petty graft or trying to make a profit, he might be given the death penalty.

Soviet leaders boasted that there were no more classes in Russia, but this was not exactly true. A new class, consisting of members of the Communist party, appeared. At the other end of the scale were the masses of peasants and workers whose standard of living remained very low.

"Confuse your enemies," became a Communist motto. This confusion, brought about by twisting the meaning of words into their opposite, aided the spread of communism. For example, when the Communists said "People's Democracy," they meant just the reverse — "Dictatorship Over the People."

Lenin died in 1924. All Russia paid him honor. His body was embalmed and placed under glass in a red granite tomb in Moscow. This has become a holy place for all Communists. It is guarded day and night by soldiers of the Red Army.

41

Two men, Trotsky and Stalin, hoped to inherit Lenin's power. Trotsky wanted to spread communism through the world with the utmost speed. Opposed to him was Stalin, the tough, quiet peasant from Russian Georgia, who wanted communism to come first to one country, Russia.

The rivalry between Stalin and Trotsky was deadly. Before his death, Lenin had said that Stalin was too rough and brutal to head the party, but the shrewd and crafty Stalin won out. Trotsky was forced into exile, where later, in 1940, he was killed in Mexico by an assassin who drove an ice pick into his head. Many people believe that Stalin was behind that killing.

From 1930 to his death in 1953 Stalin was Soviet Russia's ruthless tyrant. There was no freedom in his Russia. People lived in suspicion and fear, for no one could be sure that his neighbor was not a member of the secret police. It was a closed society.

Having established communism at home, Stalin's Russia now felt the time had come to extend it throughout the world. Russia must expand, colonize. At the same time, Stalin denounced other countries for doing what he intended to do himself.

FASCIST ITALY:
THE TYRANNY OF A SAWDUST CAESAR

It was not only the Germans who were angered by the Treaty of Versailles; the Italians, too, felt that they had been wronged. They had fought on the winning side, but where were the spoils of war? Why was Italy treated so badly? Usually warm and friendly, the Italians were now unhappy and desperate. Millions were out of work. In the cities there were strikes and riots; in the countryside, peasants seized the land, burned houses, ruined the crops. There was little to eat. Italy was ripe for revolution.

Fate gave Italy into the hands of a cocky little man with a huge chin and a bald head. Benito Mussolini (1883-1945) had a new idea, which

Mussolini welcomes his victorious legions back from Ethiopia.

Photo from European

he said would save Italy. He called it *fascism* (the word comes from the Latin *fasces*, a bundle of rods holding an ax blade, borne in ancient Roman courts as a symbol of authority).

Karl Marx had said that the history of the world was a struggle between classes, between the upper-class *aristocracy*, the middle-class *bourgeoisie*, and the working-class *proletariat*. As a young man, Mussolini had believed this. But now he said that he would force *all classes to work together under fascism* — tied together like a bundle of rods.

Soon all kinds of people — ex-soldiers, jobless workers, hungry farmers, patriotic youths, even businessmen fearful of communism — flocked to Mussolini's banners. Many joined his Fascist party. An armed Fascist militia, called the Black Shirts, roamed the streets, waging a savage civil war against the Communists. Both sides used guns, clubs, and castor oil. Castor oil was a terrible weapon — a captured enemy would be forced to drink big doses of it until he died in agony.

43

On October 26, 1922, some fifty thousand Fascists marched on Rome. A few days later Mussolini became premier of Italy.

Within a year Mussolini changed Italy into a vast prison. No Italian was allowed to leave the country. As *Duce* (leader) of army, navy, and government, Mussolini alone made the laws. He arrested or exiled all his enemies. He felt strong enough to take the blame when Giacomo Matteotti, head of the Socialist party, was murdered by Fascist bullies. He barred public meetings, fired teachers, and banned newspapers.

Mussolini knew his people well. Bullying alone would not toughen the easygoing Italians. Knowing their fondness for comic opera and the theater, he gave them a good show, complete with parades and circuses. His black-shirted Fascists strutted through the streets saluting stiff-armed like mechanical dolls. The country was plastered with signs with different slogans:

Mussolini opens an agricultural exhibit in Rome, 1933.

Photo from European

Mussolini receives the salute of his Fascist troops.

Photo from European

BELIEVE! OBEY! FIGHT!
A MINUTE ON THE BATTLEFIELD
   IS WORTH A LIFETIME OF PEACE!
CHILDBEARING IS TO THE FEMALE
   WHAT WAR IS TO THE MALE!
WAR CLEANSES!
DUCE! DUCE! DUCE!

Mussolini knew that he must have the young people on his side. They were the future. Italy was theirs, he said. The Fascist hymn was their song; it was called *Giovinezza* (Youth).

> *Youth, youth,*
> *Springtime of beauty,*
> *In fascism is the salvation*
> *Of our liberty.*

45

There were several Fascist youth groups: the Sons of the Wolf, for boys six to eight years old; the more important *Balilla,* for boys eight to fourteen years of age; the Advance Guardists, fourteen to eighteen years, and the Young Fascists, eighteen to twenty years. There were similar groups for girls. The boys were put through a hard physical training and taught to play war games. Some day they would go to war for the *Duce.* That became their aim in life.

Shouting at the top of his lungs, Mussolini told the people that in order to achieve the new Italy he planned, they must do only what he told them to do, think only what he told them to think. Above all, they must hate democracy. Democracy, he said, was a "stinking corpse."

On the practical side, Mussolini put jobless people to work in the army or on public works, such as road-building. He drained swamps to make more land for growing food. He decreed that the Italian trains must run on time. He urged mothers to have more children for the new great Italian Empire.

The *Duce* tried to give the Italian people everything except the one thing without which life is meaningless — freedom.

Prince Heinrich of Prussia is shown leaving the headquarters of his brother, Kaiser Wilhelm.

Photo from European

Mussolini's fascism lasted for only twenty-three years. The tyrant was working in the wrong century. In the old days of the Roman Empire, which he had hoped to re-create, Italy had been the center of the Western world. Now she was locked in the Mediterranean Sea, under the guns of the British fleet. Like the legendary toad, Mussolini huffed and puffed until he exploded. The Italian people learned the hard way that they had been tricked by an imitation Caesar.

At the end of World War II, the Italians who once had cheered him, turned in rage on Mussolini. They shot him and then hanged his body like a side of beef in a public square in Milan. Men, women, and children spat on his body and kicked it. It was a sickening sight, a horrible finish to Italian Fascist tyranny.

GERMANY:
FROM KAISER WILHELM II TO ADOLF HITLER

NOVEMBER 9, 1918. The once vain and boastful Wilhelm II, Kaiser of a once powerful Germany, watched helplessly as Allied guns hammered his country to destruction. There must be something he could do. He asked his army leader, General von Hindenburg for advice. The old warlord shook his head. "Your Majesty," he said, "it is hopeless. We have lost the war."

Another army commander, General Groener, put it bluntly: "Your Majesty should go to the front to seek death under the full blast of war. If you were killed, it would be the finest death possible."

Wilhelm II thought it over. He did not want to die. With one loyal companion, a little dachshund, he left secretly for Holland, to spend the rest of his life in exile.

All Germany was in chaos. Millions of young German men had been killed in the war. There was hunger in the land. The people were sick to death of turnips. Everything — coffee, cigarettes, bread — seemed to be made of those awful turnips! Workers went on strike. The sailors at Kiel rioted. The riot was the forerunner of a revolution in which not

Riot in Kiel, Germany.

Photo from European

only the Kaiser but also twenty-five rulers of German states lost their thrones.

Out of that revolution came the Weimar Republic, a democracy like those of the United States, Britain, France, and Switzerland. All citizens over twenty years of age could vote. A president was to be elected every seven years. The *Reichstag*, whose members served for four years each, made the laws. The people were at long last given a bill of rights with freedom of speech, press, and assembly.

This seemed to be the start of a new life for the Germans. But, sad to say, very few wanted the Weimar Republic. There was too much against it from the start. The Germans could never forget that it was born in the misery of defeat. And even worse, the victor powers refused to help the young republic.

Berlin housewives storm the bakeries for bread, 1937.

Photo from European

The Weimar Republic was attacked from two sides. On the Left were the Communists, who wanted a revolt on the Russian style. On the Right were the monarchists (who demanded the return of Wilhelm II and the Hohenzollern family), the militarists, the veterans, and the Fascists. How could the new republic steer a straight course between these enemies on Left and Right?

In 1923, in order to pay its debts, the government began to print more and more paper money. But paper money must have gold behind it. Without such backing, Germany's mark, once worth about twenty-five cents, began to slide in value. Soon the decline gathered speed. By November, 1923, the mark went down in value to 4,200,000,000 to the dollar. Over three hundred paper mills and two thousand printing plants worked around the clock to supply enough of the new money.

German inflation currency. This 10,000,000 mark note ($2.50) was issued by the city of Essen in 1923.

Those were mad days in Germany. All bank accounts, life insurance, and pensions became worthless. This was a topsy-turvy land of crazy money. Anyone who had a lone American dollar bill could buy a house or a nightclub or a ticket to the Kaiser's box at the opera. One woman carrying a basketful of marks went to the butcher shop to buy some meat. Because of the large crowds, she left her basket of marks on the sidewalk. When she came out, someone had dumped the marks into the gutter and had stolen the basket!

If you collect stamps, look in your album under GERMANY, 1923, WATERMARKED NETWORK. There you will see Germany's special inflation stamps. One stamp had the value of 50,000,000,000 (fifty billion) marks!

There was more trouble. A long time ago the great German poet, Goethe, had said: "May God help the German people if ever a Napoleon appears amongst them!"

Now Germany got her Napoleon. Adolf Hitler, a nervous little man with wild eyes and unruly hair, shouted to the world that he had come to save Germany. Born in the Austrian village of Braunau on April 20,

50

1889, the son of a minor customs officer, he had had a most unhappy childhood. His father beat him without mercy. In 1907 he moved to Vienna where, a flea-bitten tramp, he made a living selling postcards and working at odd jobs. "In Vienna," he later wrote, "I became a hater of Jews, an enemy of Marxism, and a German nationalist." He served in the German army in World War I, was twice wounded, earned the Iron Cross. After the war, he turned to politics.

Adolf Hitler was an evil genius. He made long-winded speeches and gave orders. He was sure that he knew all the answers to the meaning of history. He hated those who had more education than he had. He lived in a curious dreamworld, in which anyone who dared talk back to him was insane. There is little doubt that he himself was mentally unbalanced. This German Napoleon, who believed his destiny was to save Germany, was to become the greatest mass-murderer the world has ever known.

Hitler formed the Nazi, or National Socialist German Workers' Party (N.S.D.A.P.). Into the party came out-of-work war veterans, poor students, frightened businessmen, monarchists, anti-Semites, anti-Catholics, anti-liberals, and anti-Communists. A hypnotic speaker, Hitler promised something to everyone. He would put an end to the Treaty of Ver-

Adolf Hitler before his rise to power.

Photo from European

At Nuremberg, September 16, 1935, Hitler takes the salute as 100,000 Nazis march by in annual Party Day Parade.

sailles. He would get back Germany's colonies. He would drive the Jews out of the country. He would put people back to work. He would build a mighty army. He would forge a New Germany.

The brown-shirted Nazi storm troopers marched through the streets singing the "Horst Wessel Song" (named for a Nazi ruffian who had been killed by Communists):

> *The trumpet blows its shrill and final blast!*
> *Prepared for war and battle here we stand.*
> *Soon Hitler's banners will wave unchecked at last,*
> *The end of German slav'ry in our land.*

It was bitter civil war as Nazis and Communists fought each other in the streets. Many died in the bloody warfare.

Meanwhile, National Socialism continued to grow. There were several reasons for this. Hitler appealed strongly to the lower half of the middle class, which had suffered more severely than others from the inflation of 1923. The peasants, with their cattle and farms, had managed to get along. The rich had managed to hold on to their wealth. The workers had had no money to lose, and had been able to collect unemployment insurance. But the small businessmen, with their money in savings banks, the doctors, lawyers, dentists, teachers — all these had seen everything they owned wiped out overnight. They were drawn to the Nazi party, the party of hope, promises, and revenge, as to a magnet.

Nazi propaganda was clever in arousing emotions. Excitement reached a fever pitch when Hitler came to speak. Searchlights pierced the night to find his plane. Bands burst into military music. Then Hitler's magic voice went to work on his foes.

The Communist party in Germany, without knowing it, was a great help to Hitler. From Moscow, Lenin ordered the German Communists

Hitler denounces his enemies, 1940.

Photo from European

to fight both Hitler and the Social Democrats. This suited Hitler nicely; he attacked the Communists as evil internationalists.

The political situation got worse and worse. Unemployment rose, and starvation threatened. Armed bands continued to fight in the streets. Finally, on January 30, 1933, Field Marshal von Hindenburg, president of the republic he had sworn to defend, made Hitler the German Chancellor. The great general of World War I gave power to the lowly lance corporal. This was done through the behind-the-scenes work of von Papen and other aristocrats, who believed that Hitler would be a front man for them.

At the previous election the Nazis had gotten only 32 per cent of the votes, a decline from 37 per cent in 1932. Then came a stroke of great luck — the *Reichstag* fire. Who destroyed the building? "The Communists did it!" cried a thousand Nazi speakers at Hitler's order. "It was

Burning of the Reichstag, February 27, 1933.
Photo from European

Hitler, campaigning for power, is here seen in a plane together with Prince August Wilhelm, son of the former German Kaiser William II, and press agent Hanfstaengel.

Photo from European

to be a signal for their revolt!" Actually, the evidence points to the Nazis doing it themselves. A half-witted Dutchman, Marinus van der Lubbe, later executed, who helped set the *Reichstag* fire, had at one time been a Communist. But the fire broke out in several places at once. Well planned, well executed, it needed several men to start it. Some say that the real culprit was the number-two Nazi, General Hermann Goering.

Once in power, Hitler acted exactly as had Mussolini in Italy. He stamped out democracy, which he called "a system of crazy brains." He would rule alone. He made himself the *Fuehrer* (leader) of the Third Reich (empire). (The First German Reich was formed in 962 when Otto I became Holy Roman Emperor. The Second German Reich was started by Otto von Bismarck in 1871 after the fall of France in the war with Prussia. Hitler was telling the world that he was starting a great Third Empire in Germany.)

But the *Fuehrer* followed Mussolini's lead — he made all Germany a prison. He crushed his enemies, he broke up workers' unions. He set up an iron rule over every part of German life — church, press, education, industry, and army. He, and he alone, was to be the law in Nazi Germany.

Hitler lost little time in fulfilling his campaign promises. As soon as he was in power he began a vicious attack on the Jews. These people comprised only one per cent of the German people, but Hitler held them largely responsible for Germany's troubles. Before he died, Hitler had killed 6,000,000 Jews from all Europe — men, women, and children. It was one of the most hideous crimes in all history.

To Hitler the Christian religion was nonsense because of its golden rule — "Do unto others what you would have them do unto you" — and its belief in forgiveness — "Turn the other cheek." He threw pastors and priests alike into concentration camps. He gave the Germans a new god — himself; a new heaven — the Fatherland. "One Reich, One People, *One Fuehrer!*" For these they must be ready to go to war.

Hitler wanted to build for the future. "Whoever has the youth," he said, "has the future." "We older ones are rotten. But my magnificent

Marinus Van Der Lubbe, with head bowed, on trial for setting the Reichstag fire.

Photo from European

Nazi Storm Troopers picket a Jewish manufacturing firm, 1936.
Photo from European

youngsters! With them I shall make a new world." He would prepare German boys for war, educate them for victory or death.

When Hitler took over the German schools, they were among the best anywhere. He made them the worst in the world.

Like Mussolini, Hitler had a system for training the youth of Germany: the *Jungvolk* (Young Lads) from eight to fourteen, and the *Hitler Jugend* (Hitler Youth) from fourteen to eighteen. These young people were taught to take orders, to die for *Fuehrer* and Fatherland. A thirteen-year-old boy had to march eleven miles a day; a sixteen-year-old had to march fifteen and a half miles a day carrying an eleven-pound load. Many broke down on the roads. Often boys had to stay up until midnight carrying torches in Nazi parades.

The boys sang as they marched to martial music in a sea of flags:

> *We move man for man*
> *We are marching for Hitler,*
> *Through night and danger.*

Over and over again they chanted the Nazi mottoes:

THE *FUEHRER* IS ALWAYS RIGHT!
OUR LIFE FOR THE *FUEHRER*!
FREEDOM AND LIFE
    ONLY FOR THOSE READY TO FIGHT!
HEIL HITLER!

Scene on the *Ringstrasse*, Vienna, when Austria was annexed by Hitler's Germany.
Photo from European

Girls, too, were banded into clubs: Young Girls from ten to fourteen, the League of German Girls from fourteen to twenty-one. They had to learn two lessons: (1) to prepare to be a mother and bring new Nazi warriors into the world; and (2) to get ready for war.

The world has never seen anything like Hitler's Germany. The murder of millions of people, the inhuman atrocities, made it seem that the Germans had taken leave of their senses. How could they tolerate such things? This is a question that still puzzles a great many people. Was it, as one German historian has stated, a catastrophe that struck the German people like a bolt of lightning from heaven?

Certainly not! History does not work that way. Behind Hitler and nazism was a long historical tradition, a basic cause in a very complex situation. A leading state, Prussia, gradually expanded until it took over control of Germany. Its way of life became all Germany's way of life.

Prussian traits — discipline, obedience, respect for order, love for the military, worship of the leader, the State before the individual — these became German traits. Most disastrous of all was the Prussian disposition to follow and obey the leader — any leader — blindly to the death. When Hitler pushed to power, the Germans obeyed him *because he was the leader.* This was the tragic weakness of a great people. They never understood that it was suicidal to entrust their fate to a deranged *Fuehrer.*

To keep the Germans content, Hitler gave them the smell of power, a taste of glory, stolen bread, and magnificent circuses. He promised them a world empire, but he turned all Germany into a graveyard. Then, in 1945, with his empire in ruins, he fired a bullet into his own mouth.

Starved victims of the Nazi concentration camp at Evensee, Austria, following their liberation. Evensee was one of the largest of the Nazi prison camps. Inmates died at the rate of 2,000 a week.

Photo from European

Vanguard of Japanese soldiers enters Harbin, Manchuria, on February 5, 1932.
Wide World Photo

THE CHINA INCIDENT, 1931

DURING THE Long Armistice, that tragic, uneasy period between world wars, Japan emerged as an aggressor. Like Italy and Germany, Japan believed she had been denied her fair share of the world's wealth. She wanted more power, more prestige, more wealth. In 1931 she began her push into China, the first stage of aggression leading to World War II.

The Japanese emperor was highly respected by his people, but his powers were limited. The country was really ruled by a union of military leaders (sons of the old *samurai* warriors) and great financial clans called *zaibatsu*. Their eyes turned to the fertile land and rich mineral ores of the northern Chinese province of Manchuria. There was not only great wealth to be had in Manchuria, but also "living space" for the Japanese, of whom there were too many in the home islands. Since

60

A fleet of motor trucks, filled with fur-clad Japanese infantrymen, moves into Hailar, key city for Northwestern Manchuria, December 6, 1932.

Wide World Photo

Japanese emigrants were barred from Australia and the United States, why should the Japanese not overflow into Manchuria?

It was easy to find an "incident." On September 18, 1931, a small section of track on the Japanese-owned Southern Manchurian Railroad was blown up. It was only a minor explosion. The track was repaired within a few hours. But here was a reason for going to war. Japanese generals, loudly blaming the Chinese for this "cowardly attack," struck at once. In a short time the city of Mukden, with its barracks of ten thousand Chinese soldiers, was in Japanese hands. Japan then flooded Manchuria with troops.

On March 9, 1932, the Japanese set up the "Independent Republic of Manchuria," under the presidency of Henry Pu-yi, the boy emperor of China. Pu-yi had been placed on the peacock throne in Peking when he was only three years old, only to be driven out by the Chinese Revo-

61

Japanese Emperor Hirohito salutes his troops in the puppet state of Manchukuo, 1934.
Wide World Photo

lution of 1911. Now, at the age of thirty, he was made a puppet ruler by the Japanese. The new Japanese-run state of Manchukuo was not a free, "independent" nation at all.

China at once appealed to the League of Nations for help. The League set up a committee, the Lytton Commission, to look into the quarrel. The commission reported that, although Japan had special rights in Manchuria, the land would remain Chinese. Furious, the Japanese left the League of Nations and all its works and resigned from that body.

The United States, angered by Japan's moves, refused to accept the new state of affairs in Manchuria, but the rest of the world just looked the other way. The nations of the world were unwilling to get together and stop Japanese aggression. The devil's brew, they said, was always boiling over in the Far East. Why bother?

Bluff and bluster had won an easy victory. Japanese troops were in China, and the League had done nothing about it. Mussolini and Hitler learned a lesson: strike hard and strike fast; no one will do anything to stop you.

The first step toward another world war had been taken.

ITALY INVADES ETHIOPIA, 1935-36

THE NEXT GIANT STEP toward war was taken by Benito Mussolini, who needed an easy conquest to prove his strength. Mussolini took a look at Africa.

Ethiopia, or Abyssinia, an inland empire in northeast Africa, lay between two Italian lands — Italian Somaliland and Eritrea. Ethiopia was inhabited chiefly by the Amhara, who numbered two million people. These had been converted to Christianity by the Egyptian Coptic Christians. Over the centuries, however, Greeks, Jews, Arabs, and East Indians had come to Ethiopia; the kingdom was a mixture of peoples speaking over seventy different languages.

In this feudal kingdom there were many chiefs, or *rases,* who were always at war with one another. At the top was Emperor Haile Selassie, who called himself the "Lion of Judah" and the "King of Kings." He traced his ancestry to the Queen of Sheba and to Menelek, Solomon's first son.

In 1896, on the famous battlefield of Adowa, the Ethiopians, using spears and knives, had beaten an Italian army that had tried to invade their country from Eritrea. Now the *Duce* made up his mind to avenge that defeat.

First came the usual incident. On December 5, 1934, at a dreary, barren border spot called Walwal, fifteen hundred Ethiopian warriors clashed with five hundred native troops under Italian command. Men were killed on both sides. It was all Mussolini needed.

63

On October 3, 1935, while the League of Nations discussed the clash, 400,000 Italian troops advanced into Ethiopia from the north, east, and south. They were accompanied by an array of tanks, motorized units, and aircraft. They had to fight not only against the human enemy, but also against the hostile, rocky land and the brutal climate.

The Ethiopians had no big guns, no tanks, no planes; they had only primitive manpower. Their best chance was to use the hit-and-run tactics of guerrilla war against the invaders. But the *rases,* proud men, refused to behave like "bandits." They said they would stand and fight in compact mass, just as their fathers and grandfathers had done.

It was a foolish and dangerous idea, especially in view of the fact that the *rases* hated each other so much that they could not work together in common against the Italian invaders.

The war in Ethiopia was barbarous. Both sides used dumdum bullets, which break into deadly pieces on contact with the human body. When the Ethiopians found an Italian airman who had been forced down, they at once cut off his head. The Italians, in turn, sprayed fleeing Ethiopian troops with mustard gas from the air.

Vittorio Mussolini, son of the *Duce,* described the "fun" he had bombing the Ethiopians from the air:

We arrived upon them (Ethiopian cavalry) unobserved and immediately dropped our load of explosives. I remember one group of horsemen gave me the impression of a budding rose unfolding as the bombs fell in their midst and blew them up. It was exceptionally good fun.

The war lasted for seven months, until May 9, 1936. The Italians pushed slowly ahead. Haile Selassie Gugsa, drunken governor of Tigre, son-in-law of the emperor, deserted to the Italians with ten thousand men. Haile Selassie himself, defeated in April, 1936, fled on a British warship from his stricken country. The Italians then entered the capital city of Addis Ababa.

All Italy celebrated the victory. This was revenge for the shameful

Italian fascist troops enter the holy city of Aksum, Ethiopia, January, 1935.

Wide World Photo

defeat of 1896. Mussolini proudly announced to the world that Ethiopia had become a part of the Italian Empire.

The following month Haile Selassie spoke before the League of Nations at Geneva. He stood patiently waiting while Italian newsmen shouted and cursed to drown out his words, but his warning was clear:

> *I, Haile Selassie, Emperor of Ethiopia, am here to claim that justice which is due my people. . . . It is my duty to inform you of the deadly peril which threatens you. . . . It is a question of the value of promises to small states.*
>
> *Apart from the Kingdom of God, there is not on this earth any nation that is higher than any other. . . . God and history will remember your judgment.*

Conquering Italian troops are reviewed by Marshal Pietro Badoglio in the fallen capital of Ethiopia, May 28, 1936.

Haile Selassie, Negus of Ethiopia, delivers a speech before the League of Nations at Geneva. Driven out of his homeland by Mussolini's Fascists, he warns that others will suffer from fascist aggression.

Wide World Photo

The League had done its best. During the Ethiopian war, it had tried to impose sanctions (prohibition of trade) on Italy, but that had not stopped the *Duce*.

Another great stride had been taken to World War II.

THE SPANISH CIVIL WAR, 1936-39

IN THE SIXTEENTH CENTURY, with an empire circling the globe, the strongest and most feared nation in Europe was Spain. But in the twentieth century her old glory was gone. She was weak and backward, a shadow of her former self.

The Spanish were a proud people. "We are as noble as the King —

Franco's troops about to hoist their flag on the French-Spanish frontier after driving defeated Republican army from Spain.

Photo from European

only not so rich." In reality, they were poor and unhappy. Half of them could neither read nor write, and many never had enough to eat. Seven out of ten were farmers, but most had no land of their own. A few rich landlords called grandees held almost all the land. The country was ruled by a king together with the grandees, the clergy, and the juntas, or officers' councils.

Spain was one of the few countries in Europe spared the horrors of World War I. But after the war her troubles started all over again. King Alfonso XIII resigned in 1931. The Spanish Republic, set up under Niceto Alcalá Zamora, wanted to take the land from the grandees and give it to the peasants. It tried to raise wages, to give civil rights to the people, to lessen the distress.

There were two main political groups. Those who supported the republic (the Left) felt that changes were not being made fast enough.

68

Those who hated the republic (the Right) said that the revolution had gone too far too fast. Soon Spain, caught between Left and Right, was torn by riots and strikes.

At this point the Spanish Rightists, with General Francisco Franco in command, got ready for a coup d'état, a sudden blow at the state. Franco, forty-four years old, came from a middle-class home. He had spent almost thirty years in military life and had made his name known by fighting in Spanish Morocco in North Africa. Many Moors joined him as he made ready to strike at the republic.

War between Franco's Rebels and the government's Loyalists began in July, 1936. Past revolts by Spanish generals had seldom lasted more than a few months; this one raged on for almost three years.

Murder is not too strong a word to use for this cruel and bloody struggle. Loyalists and Rebels alike fought as if they were savages. On both sides there were mass killings. It was the worst kind of conflict — a civil war between brother and brother. Members of the same family were sometimes on opposing sides. No one expected mercy from the

Spanish Loyalist troops detailed to work on fortifications.
Photo from European

enemy, and neither side was content with anything less than surrender. The Fascist bombings of Madrid and Barcelona, the destruction of the town of Guernica, the first air bombings of civilians in history, horrified the democratic world.

"No pasarán!" cried the Loyalists. "They shall not pass!" A fiery, Basque-born woman, *"La Passionaria,"* urged all women to fight Franco with "knives and burning oil." Even children were caught in the evil torrent.

Mussolini's Fascist Italy and Hitler's Nazi Germany helped the Rebels. Denouncing the Loyalists as the tools of bolshevism, Mussolini and Hitler sent Franco supplies, munitions, planes, and troops (the Italians sent more than fifty thousand men).

The Russians were too far away to send troops, but they did supply the hard-pressed Loyalists with supplies and some planes during the first part of the struggle. The Russians claimed that Franco's Rebels were the agents of international fascism.

Britain and France stayed neutral and tried to keep the war from spreading, but individuals all over the world took sides. Spain became

Red militiamen on the Aragon front in Spain, December, 1936.
Photo from European

Spanish Loyalist troops haul artillery into position.

a battlefield of contending beliefs — Fascist and anti-Fascist. Thousands of persons of leftist or liberal sympathy left the United States and European countries to join an international brigade to serve with the Loyalist republican forces.

The Loyalists stubbornly held on to Madrid, even when Rebel forces pushed to the suburbs. They beat the Italians surging on Madrid from the north.

The bitter struggle came to an end on March 28, 1939. Franco and the Rebels won. Franco proclaimed himself *El Caudillo* (The Leader) and set up a Fascist rule, declaring that he had become dictator by the grace of God. He promised the king's return one day; rule by the *Falange,* his own political party; protection for the Church; a free hand to the rich; and close ties with Germany and Italy. Spain became a police state. Thousands of Loyalists, unable to escape, were killed or thrown into prison.

General Franco and his triumphant Rebel forces pursue the Loyalist troops after the fall of Barcelona.
Photo from European

Meanwhile, Dictator Franco told the world: "We do not reject democracy. We want a true democracy. But we do not want freedom to fall into anarchy. We love freedom, but freedom goes with order."

More than a million Spaniards had died in the civil war. Half the people were starving, while one out of seven was a homeless refugee. Cities and villages had been destroyed. The whole country, weak and exhausted, suffered from the old evils: low wages; grinding poverty; privileges for the few; no freedom for the many.

Worst of all, the Spanish Civil War was a curtain raiser for World War II. Its first effect was to bring Germany and Italy together. In 1936, soon after the Spanish Civil War began, Hitler and Mussolini had formed the Rome-Berlin Axis. Japan had then joined what was called the Anti-Comintern Pact — an agreement between the three powers to oppose communism. All three — Germany, Italy, and Japan — now began to push their demands with more success.

An Italian machine-gun crew attached to Franco's army.

The Spanish Civil War showed Britain and France that they were in danger. The two democratic countries had tried to keep hands off Spain — "nonintervention." This had staved off a general war, for the time being, but it meant a humiliating loss of face. And, in the long run, it pointed the way to still another, greater war because it had convinced Hitler and Mussolini that Britain and France were either too proud or too weak to fight.

HITLER TAKES THE ROAD TO WAR

WHO BEARS THE BLAME for World War I? The Allies said that Germany alone planned it for forty years. But historians today say that Germany was not the only nation responsible for that war.

73

The blame for *starting World War II rests* solely on Nazi Germany. The villain was its *Fuehrer,* Adolf Hitler. This time the record is clear. Secret reports taken from the Germans reveal that Hitler aimed to conquer all Europe. He was a threat to world peace. Obsessed with the idea that the German "race" would one day rule all mankind, he was ready to smash his way to power or to ruin.

"For the good of the German people," Hitler said, "we must wish for a war every fifteen or twenty years. If you use an army for peace you are only playing soldiers — look at Sweden or Switzerland."

Hitler wanted this war. He said he would strike down any *Schweinehund* ("pig-dog" or "filthy fellow") who stood in his way.

At the same time, Hitler was shrewd enough to tell the world: "I am not crazy enough to want a war. The German people have but one wish — to be happy in their own way and to be left in peace." Every time he chewed off another bit of land in Europe, he made a speech saying that "this is my last demand!"

While Hitler was in prison in 1923, he had written a book called *Mein Kampf* (My Battle), in which he had described how he would "break the chains of the Treaty of Versailles." Few people had believed him at the time, but they were to find out later that he had meant what he said in the bible of Nazi faith. As Hitler put his plans into effect one after the other, and as success followed success, millions of Germans who had at first thought him a comic clown began to trust him as Germany's savior.

Hitler destroyed the world's hope for peace, bit by bit. We can trace the path to World War II by watching how he did it.

In October, 1933, Hitler took Germany out of the League of Nations. He wanted the right to rearm Germany, but the League would not allow that. He turned German industry to the business of making weapons of war.

There was one brief setback in Hitler's first year of power. He went too far too quickly when he tried to take over Austria, the land of his birth. In Vienna, Austrian Nazis wounded the Austrian dictator, Engelbert Dollfuss, and watched coldly as he bled to death. Mussolini, though

Imprisoned at Landsberg before he came to power, Hitler was allowed considerable freedom. Here he is shown with visiting friends who included Rudolf Hess, second from right, who later became the number three Nazi under Hitler.

Photo from European

a friend and champion of Hitler, was furious when he heard the news. Stronger than Hitler at that time, the *Duce* did not want Germany to take Italy's neighbor. He sent Italian troops to the borders of Austria.

Hitler backed down. He would wait for another chance. One day he would attack Austria and Mussolini would do nothing about it.

In 1935 a confident Hitler announced to the world that Germany now had a strong air force. He built new naval ships and submarines. He began to draft men for the army. The Nazi star was rising again.

Hitler firmly believed that each man's destiny was controlled by the heavenly wanderings of the stars (astrology). When his astrologer told him that on March 7, 1936, his stars would be in favorable positions in the sky, Hitler sent his troops into the Rhineland. The choice of March 7 had its practical aspects, too — the date fell on Saturday, on which day the English stopped work for the traditional "long weekend." It shows Hitler's shrewdness — he made all his bold moves on Saturdays.

The occupation of the Rhineland and the other moves that followed it violated both the Treaty of Versailles and the Locarno Pact (1925), but Hitler did not care. He was certain of his destiny. When he went into the Rhineland he said, "If the French attack us, I shall commit suicide." The French did not attack.

The British and French seemed hypnotized by Hitler. They were unable to work together. Charges of double-dealing and treachery echoed back and forth between London, Paris, and Moscow, while Berlin and Rome planned more attacks.

As his enemies wavered and bickered, Hitler rearmed Germany. From 1933 to 1936 he spent $7,500,000,000 on arms, much of it on aircraft. He planned to grab neighboring lands without force if he could, but he was prepared to go to war for them. People, he said, were like animals; they were either wolves or sheep. "My German boys," he said, "have a steely glint in their eyes and daggers at their sides, and they will be as crafty and as hard and as vicious as wolves."

We Germans, Hitler reasoned on another occasion, are, along with the Italians and the Japanese, the 'have-not' people of the world. The 'have' powers, the democracies, Britain, France, and the United States, are old and bloated and flabby. Why should they have all the wealth and power? If we Germans are not given our full share, we shall go out and take it. You regard us as a bull in a china shop. What of it? Try and stop us!

Thus, while in the democracies the troops drilled with wooden guns and played at war games with tanks made of paper, Hitler built his great war machine. The records prove his guilt. At a meeting of his generals he banged on the table and shouted that he would smash anyone who opposed him. Fat Hermann Goering, the number-two Nazi, was so delighted with Hitler's tough talk of war that he jumped on top of the table and went into a war dance.

Hitler's drive for power had begun, a drive that would result in the slaughter of millions of people.

Chancellor Schuschnigg of Austria had no chance once Hitler decided to annex that country.
Photo from European

THE FALL OF AUSTRIA

ONCE AGAIN Hitler turned his eyes to Austria. Germany, he shouted, would not forget her "racial comrades" in other lands. At his signal, Nazi agitators began to riot in Vienna and other Austrian towns.

The German *Fuehrer* ordered Kurt von Schuschnigg, the Austrian chancellor, to come to see him at Berchtesgaden, his home in the mountains of Bavaria in south Germany. Hour after hour the Nazi dictator bullied his guest. He demanded that von Schuschnigg free all the Nazis jailed in Austria, give full rights to Austrian Nazis, and appoint two Nazis to the cabinet. Schuschnigg must do all this at once — or else.

Schuschnigg knew that Hitler wanted *Anschluss*, the union of Germany and Austria. Shaken, he called for a vote of all the Austrian people as to what they wanted to do. He looked to other countries for aid, but there was no help to be had. In Italy the *Duce* had gone skiing. This time it was his turn to support his fellow dictator. Had not Hitler helped him quietly in Ethiopia? Mussolini decided to say nothing.

The vote in Austria was to take place on March 13, 1938. Two days before that date a strong German army marched across the border. It soon overran the little land. By April, Austria was no longer free. A new vote, this time run by the Nazis was taken. "Do you want to become the *Ostmark*, a part of the Third Reich?" Ninety-nine point seventy-five per cent (99.75%) of the Austrian people vote *JA* (Yes).

Hitler had won a great victory in the land of his birth. At one blow he had added 7,000,000 people and another country to Germany. Back in 1934 he had promised that Austria would remain free. Once more he had broken his word.

Britain and France, although shocked by Hitler's bold move, did nothing.

Hitler on the speaker's platform at Nuremberg. To his left is Rudolf Hess.
Photo from European

THE MUNICH CRISIS

THERE WERE 3,000,000 more Germans in Czechoslovakia. Were these the "racial comrades," the remaining "captives" that Hitler had said he would set free?

Czechoslovakia was a small country set up in the heart of Europe after World War I. Once she had been a part of the old Austro-Hungarian Empire. Now she was the only real democracy in Central Europe. She had made steady progress under her first two presidents, Thomas G. Masaryk and Eduard Benes. Her industries were busy. She had become an up-to-date, thriving little country.

But Czechoslovakia was in serious trouble. She faced the German army on three sides. For half her length she was caught in a pincers formed by the German and Austrian borders. Look at the map. Note how Czechoslovakia was trapped in the jaws of the German wolf's-head. If the German wolf closed its mouth, it could cut Czechoslovakia into two pieces.

Hitler wanted those Germans who lived in the Sudetenland to return to Germany. That area had never belonged to Germany. The Germans who lived there had always been treated well by the Czechs. But their Nazi leader, Konrad Henlein, said: "We wish to be home in the Reich."

In March, 1938, a week after he took Austria, Hitler turned to Czechoslovakia. "Our German brothers," he shouted over the radio to his people, "are being killed!" Either the Sudeten Germans were set free by September or he would march with his troops into Prague, capital of Czechoslovakia.

Again the democracies froze. The French, who had a treaty with Czechoslovakia, said that their army was in no condition to go beyond its own borders. The Soviet Union said that it would fight if France did. But France would not move without Britain. And the British had no desire to go to war. Finally, the British and the French decided to appease Hitler. They would calm him by giving in to his demands, and there would be peace.

Prime Minister Neville Chamberlain of Britain, armed with an umbrella, got into a small plane and made the first flight of his life. He flew to Germany to see Hitler. He told the Nazi leader that he would agree that the Sudeten Germans could vote whether or not they wanted to be taken over by Germany.

Hitler was furious. This was not enough for him. He felt cheated of his war. He massed his troops on the Czech border.

It was a moment of almost total despair for the democracies. There had been twenty years of peace. Now another war was nearly at hand.

Then, of all people, Mussolini stepped in as savior. He said he was ready to meet with Hitler, Daladier (the French premier), and Chamberlain to discuss the issue. All agreed that this was the best way to bring about a peaceful settlement.

The brief meeting was held at Munich, in south Germany, where the Nazi movement had begun. All Hitler's demands were met. The Czechs were betrayed by their friends. Hitler gained eleven thousand square miles of land rich in industry, electric power, and military posts.

The *Fuehrer* had won again, and the Germans were happy that they had not had to fight for the victory. Hitler said, "I have no more demands in Europe."

In London a vast crowd waited at the airport to greet Chamberlain. The prime minister, smiling, held up and waved the paper that Hitler had signed at Munich.

"I return from Germany," said Chamberlain, "bringing peace with honor."

But he had brought back neither peace nor honor. Within another year Britain would be at war with Germany.

THE HITLER-STALIN PACT, AUGUST 23, 1939

ADOLF HITLER had won two amazing victories. Without firing a shot he had taken over Austria and the mountain strongholds of Czechoslovakia. But he was greedy for more. In the streets the Nazi bullyboys shouted: "TODAY GERMANY: TOMORROW THE WORLD!"

The *Fuehrer* had always said that Germany must have more *Lebensraum* (living space). Austria and Czechoslovakia, apparently, did not meet the demand. Where would Hitler turn this time? Most people guessed that Poland would be next. But after Poland? All Europe, perhaps. And after that?

The problem of the moment was Poland. Hitler turned first to the city of Danzig (Gdansk), which, after World War I, had been placed under control of the League of Nations. Not only did he want Danzig, but also that strip called the Polish Corridor which separated the two parts of Germany. The Poles refused to give up an inch of their land.

Then the Nazi radio went into noisy action. "We shall free our German brothers in Poland!" "The Poles are animals!" "Down with the Poles!" "*Heil* Hitler!"

All the world knew what this meant. It was too much for Prime Minister Chamberlain. He had gone out of his way to trust Hitler. Now he had had enough of Germany and her lying *Fuehrer*. Britain, France, and Poland signed a pact saying they would fight if any one of them was attacked. There it was, plain for all to see — if Hitler moved on Poland, he would have to go to war with Britain and France. This time there were no "ifs" and "buts."

What about Soviet Russia? What would Joseph Stalin, the Red dictator, do now? He hated both Hitler and Chamberlain. But he was most suspicious of Chamberlain. Had not the British prime minister flown to Germany to appease Hitler at Munich? Would the British consent to a second Munich and leave the Russians open to attack at the last moment?

Hitler feared a war on two fronts — in the West against Britain and France, and in the East against Soviet Russia. True, he despised the Russians, but he could gain by joining them. If he made a bargain with Stalin, he would remove the threat in the East, at least for the time being. He would act on one front at a time. And later on he would settle accounts with "those filthy Russians."

Stalin, on his part, hated and feared the Nazis. He believed that the British and the French were trying to turn Germany against Russia so that they would destroy each other. Stalin decided that if the democracies would not do business with him, he would do business with the Nazis.

On August 23, 1939, Germany and Russia signed a pact agreeing not to go to war against each other for ten years. At the same time they made a second, secret pact splitting all of Poland between Germany and Russia.

WORLD WAR II BEGINS

THE HITLER-STALIN pact gave the green light to the Nazis in Poland. The drums began to roll again in the German press and over the radio. "The Poles are beating our German brothers!" Hitler said the question of Poland must be settled at once.

The skies darkened that summer. In vain did the British and French tell Hitler that they would see what they could do about German

As World War II begins, endless lines of Poles wind through the streets of Warsaw to escape the invading Nazis, September, 1939.

Photo from European

charges against the Poles. Hitler was now secure in the East, where he no longer feared the Russians would attack him. Let the West beware!

The blow came on September 1, 1939. Without declaring war, Hitler sent his troops across the borders of Poland. They smashed in with speed and fury. It was the first *Blitz* (lightning) attack of the war. So swift was the German rush on land and in the air that the Poles never had a chance.

Fifty hours later, as they had promised, Britain and France declared war on Germany. The Long Armistice was ended. World War II had begun.

83

INDEX

85

World War I, 1
  cost of, 1-2
  heritage of, 1-3
  Maginot Line, 13
  manpower losses in, 1
  peace treaty (*see* Treaty of Versailles)
  spoils of, 7
  See also France; Germany; Italy; Russia
  cause of (*see* Germany; Hitler, Adolf)

invasion of Poland and, 82-83
  See also France; Great Britain; Italy;
    Spanish Civil War (1936-39); Union of
    Soviet Socialist Republics (USSR)

Yugoslavia, 13
Young Communist League (*Komsomol*), 40

Zaibatsu, 60
Zamora, Niceto Alcalá, 68